You'll Have Had Your Hole

From the writer of *Trainspotting* comes a chemical-age horror, a deeply unsettling tale for the '90s.

Within the sound-proofed walls of a disused recording studio, a score is being settled. Two inner city low-lifes take the law into their own hands to satisfy their craving for fun, fear and a freakish sense of justice.

Irvine Welsh lives in Edinburgh. *Trainspotting*, his first book, was published in 1993 to instant acclaim. It was subsequently adapted for the stage and first performed at the Citizens Theatre, Glasgow, in 1995. *Headstate*, developed with the Boilerhouse Theatre Company, was first performed at the Lemon Tree Theatre, Aberdeen, in 1994. His other novels include *The Acid House*, *Marabou Stork Nightmares* and *Ecstasy*.

by the same author

Trainspotting (novel)
Marabou Stork Nightmares (novel)
The Acid House (novella and short stories)
Ecstasy (novel)
Trainspotting & Headstate (plays)

for a complete catalogue of Methuen Drama write to:

Methuen
Random House
20 Vauxhall Bridge Road
London SW1V 2SA

Irvine Welsh

You'll Have Had Your Hole

Methuen Drama

First published in Great Britain in 1998 by Methuen
Random House, 20 Vauxhall Bridge Road, London SW1V 2SA

Random House Australia (Pty) Limited
20 Alfred Street, Milsons Point, Sydney,
New South Wales 2061, Australia

Random House New Zealand Limited
18 Poland Road, Glenfield, Auckland 10, New Zealand

Random House South Africa (Pty) Limited
Endulini, 5A Jubilee Road, Parktown 2193, South Africa

Random House UK Limited Reg. No. 954009

A CIP catalogue record for this book
is available from the British Library

Papers used by Random House UK Limited are natural,
recyclable products made from wood grown in sustainable forests.
The manufacturing processes conform to the environmental
regulations of the country of origin.

ISBN 0 413 72860 9

Typeset by Deltatype Ltd, Birkenhead, Merseyside
Printed and bound in Great Britain by
Cox & Wyman Ltd, Reading, Berkshire

Introduction

It's very difficult to examine your own motivation in undertaking any piece of creative writing. In the case of my new play, however, I decided upon medium before content, electing to write a play, simply because I'd never written one before. It seemed a logical step; I'd done novels, novellas, stories, songs and poems; I'd adapted and produced original screenplays and developed *Headstate*, a performance piece with Boilerhouse Theatre Company. The conventional stage-play seemed the next thing to tackle.

After the original stage adaptation of my novel *Trainspotting*, Ian Brown, who directed the piece, and who was at the time the artistic director at the Traverse Theatre in Edinburgh, asked me if I fancied writing a play for him. At the time I was new to the writing game and was still trying to come to terms with the idea that people might actually like what I'd done.

So after satisfying myself that he wasn't taking the piss, I told Ian that I would like to at some point but it wasn't on my immediate agenda. The idea was appealing, though, and I resolved to have a crack at it when I got the time. Three years later when I called him out of the blue with a 'remember that play you wanted . . ?', I suppose that it was Ian's turn to be surprised, even if he was far too urbane to show it.

Being involved, if only minimally, in the *Trainspotting* play, gave me an opportunity to work with different people. I find that success is only something you can value if it's shared. I tend to get a much bigger buzz from being part of a team working in music, cinema or theatre than I do from writing a book, which I still tend to think of more as a lucrative hobby than real work. Also, with a play, the press and promotional side is shared with other artistic staff, while with the novel the entire focus is on you.

This suits me as I hate doing interviews; because basically, more often than not, I haven't got anything interesting to say. As a result, I always feel a bit daft after the subsequent manufacturing of passions, which you invariably get into doing when you're asked to focus on something you're not in the habit of thinking about. So the more actors, directors, etc. available to share that burden, the better.

The good news for any novelists considering writing a play is that it should be well within your capabilities. Writing a play is a lot easier than writing a novel, but only if you can appreciate the difference between the mediums and the role of the other people involved in the creative team. It means coming down from a position of near omnipotence to being somebody who is prepared to relinquish that power. That's the important rider, and that's why, I feel, many novelists fail as playwrights or screenwriters.

So why is writing a play intrinsically easier than doing a book? Well, for a start, you only need to fill up about 100 pages, rather than anything from around 180 to 500, which most novels are expected to come in at. However, you still have to *think* about considerably more than that. With stage and screenwriting, what you leave out is as important as what you put in. My first efforts for stage and screen were over-wordy, ponderous affairs with copious stage directions.

In short, I was trying to do the director's job and also to programme the actors as if they were robots. In retrospect I can see how patronising and absurd this was, but I think there must be a tendency for novelists to want to dot all 'i's and cross all 't's when they switch to stage-writing. F. Scott Fitzgerald wanted to be a screenwriter but his efforts in that direction were reputedly terrible. It was said he fell into the trap of offering far too many details – which of course are the actors', directors' and designers' jobs.

The hardest thing for a writer to do is to accept that his or her effort is emphatically not the play or the movie. It's merely an enabling document to allow those outputs to be produced. Every line you write can't be regarded as sacrosanct. You have to be prepared to enter into a different set of relationships. While the novelist is isolated but largely omnipotent (at least until the editor has his say) the stage or screenwriter is part of a team. They may be Prime Minister when the writing is taking place, but they soon relinquish this role to the director during the staging or filming part of the process. (John Hodge who wrote *Shallow Grave* and adapted *Trainspotting* for screen memorably likened the role to that of a constitutional monarch. You'll get consulted, but that's about it – which is exactly as it should be.)

If you're a control freak (and I suspect a lot of novelists might be) then you really will save yourself a lot of pain by thinking carefully beforehand as to whether or not this is for you. A novelist I know once publicly threatened a theatre director with a 'glassing', so distraught was this person about the way the director had 'destroyed' his play.

It all goes back to my man-management guru John Adair's principles of action-centred leadership. While writing a novel you can be task-orientated, while in writing a play you have to be just as concerned with the maintenance of relationships, as the accomplishment of the task is contingent on this.

For me, one of the best things about writing a play is the creative assistance from other people in terms of input. The National Theatre were kind enough to provide space and to pay for a group of actors, Tam Burn, Kenny Bryans, Susan Vidler and Malcolm Shields, to help me develop the characters and the script.

I'm used to working with people, and for that reason I could never just sit at the word processor and stick to stories and novels. Playing God can be a lonely business. I'd go crazy and I probably would end up taking as many drugs as some people assume I do. Playwriting and screenwriting suits me. Then, when you get sick of the hassle and want to do your Greta Garbo bit, that empty desk and chair in your office will always be waiting for you.

Of course, there's a downside: while writing a novel prepares you well for doing a play, unfortunately the reverse isn't true. Playwriting or screenwriting can seriously damage your health as a novelist. I was recently forced to come to terms with the fact that my last book wasn't up to the standard of the first three, particularly the one preceding it. After pondering why this was, I eventually put the blame squarely on the fact that I'd been writing screenplays just before doing the book. I think I was still stuck in screenwriting mode when I was doing it, and as a result much of the writing is too sparse and cold.

So on to the play. I conceived of *You'll Have Had Your Hole* as I was hanging around recording studios with my band Hibee Nation. Time tends to fly past in such an environment where you only really leave to go to the off-licence, pub or curry house. In short, it's a perfect black-box setting; a tight claustrophobic, closed world.

It's not too hard to imagine some grisly things going on there. I'd been taking an interest in Shakespearian and Greek tragedies and they melded with this environment largely dictating the content of the play. Out of respect to my music mates Kris, Sarah, Wonder and Henry, I'd better add that they behave a lot better at Hibee Nation recording sessions than the characters in *You'll Have Had Your Hole* do. (Well, most of the time.)

I didn't do much research in the way of attending plays. The ambience of most theatres doesn't really appeal to me. Maybe it's just a guilty conscience but I always feel as if I've stolen something in those sort of places. I'm just waiting for the hand on the shoulder. Part of the thrill of *Trainspotting* and *Headstate* for me was in seeing all that change. When I went to see *Trainspotting*, the start of the play was delayed because the box office was so used to dealing with people who had credit cards, all the punters turning up with cash flummoxed them. It was interesting to see a crowd come and get tanked up on lager and unselfconsciously get up in the middle of the play to go to the toilets.

I tried to get in to see *Shopping and F—ing* but it was always sold out. Maybe next time. The one play I did get to see last year was Ben Elton's *Popcorn* which I enjoyed very much. I had a problem with the first couple of acts because it seemed to that the old British uses of irony and satire had problems getting to grips with the hyper-realism of the Tarantino-type characters. (It's hard to satirise something that already parodies itself in an over-the-top way.) Those reservations were blown away by the third act, which resolved the issues of the play with what I could only describe as a piece of dramatic genius. What I (hopefully) got from that is that if you build up to a dramatic climax, it had better be a good one.

If the play is not a success, then, it'll be down to me. A good script is a necessary, if not sufficient, element for a good play or film. I say this as I know the cast is excellent and well up for it, and the support from Ian Brown and the West Yorkshire Playhouse has been brilliant, *You'll Have Had Your Hole* is already scheduled for Helsinki, Lisbon and Barcelona before coming to London.

I'm highly delighted that it's going to Leeds first. Apart from anything else, it's a good opportunity to hang out with those legendary party animals, the Back To Basics crew. We'll all have a good time and a few top nights out and you can't ask for much more, can you? Mind you; I suppose a successful play would be a nice bonus.

Irvine Welsh,
February 1998

You'll Have Had Your Hole

You'll Have Had Your Hole was first performed at the West Yorkshire Playhouse, Leeds, on 19 February 1998. The cast was as follows:

Dex	Malcolm Shields
Laney	Kirsty Mitchell
Docksey	Billy McIlhaney
Jinks	Tam Dean Burn

Directed by Ian Brown

Characters

Dex, *a small-time gangster who has been kidnapped by two other small-time gangsters.*
Laney, *Dex's girlfriend.*
Docksey, *one of the small-time gangsters who has kidnapped Dex.*
Jinks, *Docksey's partner.*

Note

The play is set in Edinburgh. It concerns the fortunes of Dex, who is kidnapped and imprisoned in a old recording studio. The kidnappers are Docksey and Jinks, two boyhood friends who are both undergoing personal crises. They kidnap Dex to settle a personal score. Laney, Dex's girlfriend, becomes involved in this scenario. Dex, Docksey and Jinks are three working-class men from Edinburgh. Laney comes from somewhere outside of the city.

The National Theatre provided valuable resources to develop the play in March 1997. Thanks to them. Special thanks to the staff at the West Yorkshire Playhouse (who were magic), all the staff involved in the production of the play, Susan Vidler and Kenny Bryans. Special thanks to Ian Brown and Tam, Kirsty, Billy and particularly Malcolm (sooner you than me, mate.) Also, a big nice one to Dave and Vicky and all the crew at Back To Basics for looking after me. Always a pleasure.

Scene One

An abandoned recording studio. The building is soundproofed and has scaffolding fixtures on the roof for lighting. This is the main space for the performers to record. Off this is a glass booth where the controls are situated. **Dex** *is a prisoner in the studio. He is chained up to the scaffolding with both his arms dangling from the roof. In front of* **Dex** *the studio has been furnished with a couch, a television and a coffee table. A mobile phone sits on the table.*

Dex Whair am ah! Somebody! Get me fuckin oot ay this! Help ays! Some cunt! See when ah git oot ay here some cunt dies! Ah'm fuckin well tellin yis! Yis dinnae ken whae yis'uv fuckin well goat here! Dex Murray!
Ah've fuckin well done nowt!
What dae yis want wi me? Ah ken the fuckin rules ay the game! Ah sais nowt! Ah've always kept ma mooth shut! Laney . . .
Laney.

Enter **Docksey** *and* **Jinks**. *Ignoring* **Dex**, *they are dancing conga-style and singing a song from a Barbara Stanwyck musical.*

Docksey/Jinks De yellow gold on de tree, de banana, de yellow gold on de tree, de banana . . .

Dex Get ays fuckin well oot ay here!

Docksey *and* **Jinks** *still ignore* **Dex**.

Docksey Aw fuck . . . some night, eh?

Dex Ah'm fuckin well tellin yis!

He is looking at **Docksey** *particularly, as if in recognition.*

Youse cunts! Fuckin listen tae me!

Jinks A'hm speedin oot ma box. What videos are there? What aboot that John Woo?

Docksey Sound . . .

He adopts a Kung Fu stance.

... wah wah ooh ooh say you players mulahfluckah ...

Jinks *puts a video in, and he and* **Docksey** *sit down on the couch.*

Dex   Git this fuckin oaf me! Ah'm fuckin well tellin yis!

Jinks   Hud oan ... ah thoat ah heard somethin.

Docksey   Surely not, Jinks, ma auld mucker. This building is completely soundproofed. An old recording studio. Aw sorts could go oan doon here, n nae cunt wid be any the wiser.

Jinks   Aw sorts ...

Dex   Youse two dinnae ken who yir fuckin aboot wi!

Jinks   Yes, Docksey, I'm definitely picking up some interference on the airwaves.

Docksey *turns to* **Dex** *and points at him as if seeing him for the first time.*

Docksey   Ah ha! And what have we here!

Jinks   Hello, little sweetheart. What's your name?

Jinks *strolls around* **Dex**, *evaluating, nodding his head, then stopping behind him.*

Dex   What the fuck dae youse want! Whae the fuck are youse!

Docksey (*to* **Dex**)   Still no mind ay ays mate? (*To* **Jinks**.) This is Dex. (*To* **Dex**.) This is Jinks, my long-time associate.

Jinks *moves round to face* **Dex**.

Jinks   I'm called Jinks because I'm a cat.

He hisses and claws the air.

I hate those meeces to peeces. Git it!

He tickles **Dex** *then walks around him, looking him over.*

Ye never telt me this cunt was so fuckin pretty. I didn't get a good look at him last night. I shouldn't have hit him so hard. Did I hurt your sweet face, angel heart? Eh?

Dex   You fuckin gubbed me wi that bat! You! You're fuckin deid, mate! You dinnae ken whae yir fuckin wi!

He turns to **Docksey**. *He obviously knows him but is unwilling to acknowledge this.*

You ... you ... Let me go!

Jinks   Hud oan ... hud oan ... you've goat me a wee bit confused here. You sais ah wis deid.

He turns to **Docksey**.

Docksey, there wis me feelin oan toap ay the world as well. Awright, so ah have a wee bit ay a ... condition. Yes, ah took a wee bit too much speed at the club. But deid ... nup, ah dinnae feel deid.

Docksey *puts his ear to* **Jinks**'s *chest.*

Docksey   No, Jinks, yir in perfect health ma auld mucker. I think Dex is indulging in a spot of wish fulfilment.

Dex   Ah'm warnin youse ...

Docksey *grabs* **Dex** *by the throat and squeezes.*

Docksey   Listen for a wee second here, Dex. You're telling us that you're a hard cunt who nobody messes with, right?

Dex *is silent.* **Docksey** *turns to* **Jinks**.

Docksey   That was the gist of what Dex was saying, I believe.

Jinks   I picked that up.

Docksey   You also gave us the impression that you intended to do us some harm when we released your fuckin scabby little erse from captivity.

Jinks (*to* **Dex**)   I believe that was what you said, sweet blouse.

Docksey Your behaviour isnae really convincin us that you are overendowed with grey matter, Dex.

Jinks (*winks*) I'm sure you make up for that lack of endownment in other areas though. Eh?! Eh?!

Docksey Dex, if 'A': you are a hard cunt, and I for one am not convinced you're half the man you say you are, I cite our ease in overpowering you, even with the element of surprise in our favour, and bringing you here, but assuming I'm wrong and you are, and 'B' you are going to kill us ...

Jinks ... by revealing that information to us, you have totally destroyed any incentive we may have had of releasing you.

Docksey You know why we brought you here, Dex? Eh?

Docksey *releases* **Dex** *from the grip.*

Dex Fuck off! Ah dinnae ken youse cunts!

Docksey Aw fuck, he's still playing games, still pretending that he doesnae ken me. Rude fucker, eh, Jinks?

Jinks That's the problem with a lot of pretty people. We think that we can treat the rest of the world like dirt. And we're right, Dex. Or we're usually right. But no this time.

Dex Ah'm fuckin warnin youse ...

Docksey He was up town with his girlfriend last Friday there, and I recognised him as an old colleague and said hello. You ken what he did, Jinks, what this cunt here did, did tae *me*?

Jinks No, pray tell, pray tell.

Docksey He snubbed me. The other week. I goes: Dex! Awright, mate. Heard ye were back in toon. That's what I said. This cunt though, you know what he turns roond and says?

Jinks No-oo-oo ...

Docksey He said: Dae ah ken you, mate? That was

what he said. I just thought, so that's it, eh, and ah walked away.

Jinks Ah bet you felt hurt.

Dex So that's it. Well, look mate, ah dinnae ken you! Ah say nowt. If ye ken me, ye ken that.

Jinks Manners maketh the man.

He goes round behind **Dex.**

A lovely arse on him. A real boy-arse.

Dex Eh . . .

Docksey How is it that you poofs ewywis say a boy-arse, when the arse is actually quite feminine, like Dex's.

Jinks *smiles and keeps looking at* **Dex.**

Dex Listen, you cunt's've proved yir fuckin point. Now what is it that ye want? People'll be lookin for me. People you wouldnae like tae meet.

Docksey I think you know as well as me that we've already met those people.

He shakes his head and laughs and switches on a tape recorder.

Anything you say will be taken down . . .

Dex *notes this and is silent.*

Docksey What we want is tae get tae know you, Dex. We just want ye tae tell us all about yersel. It's as simple as that, my friend.

Jinks (*singing, in* **Dex***'s ear*) Getting to know you . . .

Dex You cunts are fuckin deid! Ah'm tellin yis, yir fuckin dead meat ya fuckin sick fuckin arseholes . . .

Jinks What was that?

He rewinds the tape.

Dex (*taped voice*) You cunts are fuckin deid! Ah'm tellin yis, yir fuckin dead meat ya fuckin sick fuckin arseholes . . .

Jinks *adjusts the tape making the voice go squeaky.*

Dex (*taped voice*) ...ya sick fuckin arseholes ... ya sick fuckin arseholes ...

Jinks *puts the tape back on record.*

Docksey We must speak fuckin nice though, Dex. We don't want to listen to this foul language.

Jinks *pulls* **Dex***'s head back by the hair, and* **Docksey** *stuffs a ball-gag into his mouth. They secure it with straps from the back.*

Docksey Look, Dex, don't be making any long-term plans, because you're going to be here for a while. It's going to be quite a miserable time, in fact it's going to be the worst. We can't guarantee that we won't torture you at any time. The truth is that we might just torture you for fun, even if you do co-operate ...

Jinks *has produced a pair of long-nosed pliers and is holding them menacingly.*

Jinks ...but it won't be personal, if we're just doing it for fun, it'll simply be because of the pleasure it gives us, rather than cause of anything you've done wrong. It might no really sound it, angel heart, but that's far better than us doing it because you've annoyed us. There's a nastier edge to it then, and it's less easy to negotiate with us.

Docksey Try to relax those facial muscles, Dex.

Jinks He's going quite red.

Docksey Breath slowly and evenly through the nose. Don't fight it, feel it. Think of your girlfriend. Laney. Is that short for Lorraine? Bet ye it is. Quite young, Dex. She'll be worried aboot ye. Up in that wee flat on her ain. But I'll see that she gets taken care of awright. I won't be ungentlemanly and ask if she's a good ride, I'll find out myself soon enough. Aw aye, ah plan tae check her oot.

He picks up the mobile phone and taps it in the palm of his other hand. He and **Jinks** *are walking around* **Dex***, circling him like vultures.*

Thing is, ah wonder just how heartbroken she'll be aboot your disappearance. Ah'll have tae use her, Dex, use her tae find out aboot you. As you say yirsel, yir no a great talker ... although that's mibbe no the case ...

He stares at **Dex** *who does not meet his eyes.*

... mibbe she'll tell ays what ah need tae ken. I'll bit eftir a session wi me, she'll forget aw aboot you. I'll bet she's a slag like that, Dex: always wi the guy that's goat the wad in his wallet. Ah ken the type: I'll bet she fuckin well takes it aw weys.

Jinks Ever been wi another guy, Dex? I'll bet you wouldnae be able tae get enough ay it once ah've shown ye the ropes.

Dex *is mumbling through the gag.*

Docksey Whoa, Dex! In here for just a few ooirs and on a promise already! What a fuckin machine!

Jinks (*imitating* **Dex**) Mmm mmm mmm ... you no even manage to be dignified in silence?

Docksey He's still got that hate in his eyes, Jinks. Hopefully that'll turn to fear, and then love. He's still Dex the hardcunt. He's still in role. Problem is, there's a new script for the cunt tae learn here. Ah ken what you're thinking, Dex: we've made a terrible mistake, Fat Tyrone'll kill us when he hears aboot this.

Dex *looks downcast.*

Jinks Aw ... he didnae like that one! Fat Tyrone.

Docksey There's a name tae play wi, Dex. One ay they people ye dinnae want tae meet, eh? Ah'll let you think aboot it. Anywey, back tae John Woo! Get ays in the mood for some Woo-ing later on oan. Wi your bit ay fanny!

Jinks C'moan, Docksey ... fuck John Woo the now. Stick oan that tape. John Digweed ya cunt!

Docksey That would be sound. Ah dinnae think ah

could settle n watch a movie wi aw this speed coarsin through me. We should really ask Dex his view though. What's it tae be, Dex? Tape or film?

Dex *is silent.* **Jinks** *grabs his hair and removes his gag.*

Jinks   Tape or fuckin film ya fuckin rude cunt?

Dex   Fuck off! Dae what yis fuckin like!

Docksey *switches on a tape.*

Docksey   Consensus for the tape.

Jinks *puts the ball-gag back on to* **Dex**. *Public Image is blaring out from John Digweed's dance mix.*

Docksey   Just think, Dex, those wee nostrils ay yours. Taking in aw that sweet air.

Jinks   It's just those two little holes that stand between you and oblivion. They have to be kept clear at all times, those wee tunnels of life.

He pinches **Dex***'s nose shut for an indecently long time. As he releases it he sticks a bottle of amyl nitrate under it.*

Perty time!

Dex *twists and writhes in his bonds.*

Jinks *and* **Docksey** *laugh and dance off the speed.* **Docksey** *turns to* **Dex** *with a clenched fist.*

Docksey   Fuckin kickin in here the night, eh Dex? Glcd ye could fuckin well join us!

Scene Two

Laney *is in* **Dex***'s flat. She is dressed in footballer's girlfriend skanker mode: high-street trendy, fake tan, waxed legs. She is moving restlessly and aimlessly around the flat, from the window back to the couch, putting different Northern Soul tapes on and off.*

Laney   Where are you, ya bastard! Treat me like a fuckin

ornament, then vanish off the face of the earth leavin me wi nothing!
Selfish bastard . . . selfish fuckin bastard.

She looks at **Dex**'s *picture.*

Ah'm no gaunny be your fuckin slave! Ah've no fuckin money! Ah cannae even go oot! You've left me wi nae fuckin money! Ah fuckin hate you! Ah fuckin hate you! Nothing!
Ah'm fuckin skint!

The phone rings and she picks it up. The stage goes dark. **Laney** *and* **Jinks** *are picked out of the darkness, talking on the phones.*

Laney Hello?

Jinks Hello. I want to speak to Dex.

Laney Ah dunno whaire eh is. Ehs no been in. Eh husnae even phoned.

Jinks Fuck! Eh wis supposed tae be working wi me last night!

Laney Who's this?

Jinks My name's Rab Jenkins. Jinks. Eh hud tae meet ays last night. Eh never showed up. Whaire is the cunt!

Laney Ah don't know! Ehs no phoned! When ehs workin away eh eywis phones! Ah've no seen um!

Jinks When ye do, be sure n tell un tae phone Jinks. And dinnae you leave the hoose until ye hear fi um. Fir yir ain sake.

Laney What dae ye mean! Ah cannae stey in! Ah've nae money! Ah don't know anybody round here!

Jinks Ah'll send somebody round wi money. He'll tell ye what tae dae. Mind though, if Dex comes back, tell um tae phone Jinks. Straightaway.

Laney Ah cannae stey here wi nae money . . .

Jinks Ah'll sort that oot. You stey put n ah'll call ye back in a bit. Dinnae answer the door tae any cunt. Right?

Laney   Ah'm no in any kind ay trouble am ah?

Jinks   Just dinnae answer the door. Better safe thin sorry.
Ah mean, Dex wisnae in any kind ay trouble, now he's
fuckin vanished. You jist stey in until ah call back.

Laney   Right . . .

The spotlight goes from **Laney** *and she exits.*

The spotlight stays on **Jinks** *for a bit. He puts the phone down.*

Jinks   That slag's well fuckin rattled.

The lights go up and **Jinks** *and* **Docksey** *are seen to be in the
control room.*

I was so-oh masterly. Now we have a real damsel in
distress. She needs a knight in shining armour.

He looks at **Docksey**. **Docksey** *looks at himself and puts on an
American accent.*

Docksey   But where could we find such a man?

*They both laugh in a nasty, sinister manner, delighting in their shared
power over* **Laney**, *and through her,* **Dex**.

Jinks *and* **Docksey** *then come dancing from the control area into
the main studio where* **Dex** *is restrained.* **Docksey** *crashes out on
the couch.*

Docksey (*singing*)   What a swell party this is . . .

Jinks *goes over to* **Dex**. *He is always walking behind him, just
slightly out of his range of vision. He picks up a pair of sharp
scissors from the table.*

Jinks   You look a wee bit hot. I'm going to take off that
nice T-shirt.

He cuts **Dex**'s *T-shirt.*

Don't struggle, angel cake, I might just cut you . . . there
. . . oooh . . . Mister Ripped T-shirt 1998 . . . that's better.
The circulation of air, eh.

Docksey *moves over to the controls and starts mucking around for a bit. Then he goes to* **Dex** *and removes his gag as* **Jinks** *admires his handiwork.* **Jinks** *then puts the scissors down and picks up the pliers.*

Docksey   That better?

Dex   Look . . . what is it ye want?

Docksey   An answer tae a simple question. I asked ye if that was better.

Dex   Fuck off!

Jinks *pinches* **Dex** *in the tits with the pliers.*

Dex   Aaggghhhhh!!!

Jinks   Answer the question, angel heart or I'll hurt you very badly.

Dex   Aye . . . it's better . . .

Docksey   Who do you prefer? Marvin Gaye or George Benson?

Dex   What?

Docksey *hits* **Dex** *in the face.*

Docksey   Wrong! Who do you prefer, Marvin Gaye or George Benson?

Dex   Eh . . .

Docksey *moves forward.*

Dex   . . . awright! Ah dinnae ken . . . ah mean . . . George Benson . . .

Docksey   Wrong!

Docksey *punches* **Dex** *hard in the stomach, then starts securing the gag, but* **Jinks** *pushes him away.*

Jinks   Fuck off! Ah like George Benson!

Dex   Youse are fuckin deid!

Docksey   Well ah fuckin like George Benson. But we're comparin George fuckin-disco-jazz-funk Benson tae the greatest soul artist that ever fuckin well lived. George fuckin-easy-listening-handbags-oan-the-disco-flair Benson.

Dex   Ah'm fuckin tellin yis!

They still ignore **Dex.**

Jinks   Naw naw man, you asked my sweetcake for his honest opinion and he gave it.

Docksey   C'moan tae fuck, Jinks. You're no tryin tae tell me that Benson's in the same fuckin league as Marvin Gaye?

Dex   Youse cunts . . .

Jinks   All I'm saying, is that under Scots Law the verdict must be one of not proven.

Docksey   Awright . . . awright. Accepted. You want tae build a nice cosy relationship wi Dex here, and ah think that's as cool as fuck. Because ah'm oot oan the prowl.

He turns to **Dex.**

Will ah tell ye where ah'm off tae, will ah, Dex? Ah'm off tae see Laney. Ah'm off for some sexual healing. (*Sings.*) Come on come on, come on come on let's make love tonight . . .

Jinks   Well, I'll sit with Dex here and have a quiet night in. I'll feed you Chinese, Dex. Do you like Chinese? You rike Tynese?

Dex   Listen, ah'm fuckin warnin you, you'd better no touch Laney!

Docksey *shakes his head dismissively.*

Docksey   You think ah'm a fuckin rapist? Ah might be a loot ay things but ah'll never be that. She'll want it, man. She'll want it. You dinnae understand women; George fuckin Benson. Dickheid!

Dex (*shouts*)   Let me fuckin go! Help! Help!

Jinks *and* **Docksey** *improvise Lulu's 'Shout'.*

Jinks *and* **Docksey** *laugh together.* **Docksey** *goes and plays back some of* **Dex**'s *screams. He slows it down and speeds it up.*

Docksey   I love getting creative in the studio.

Jinks *goes to the table and picks up two sharp knives.*

Jinks   So do I! (*Laughs, then puts on Surrey record-producer accent.*) There's always such excitement when Dex's hanging around the studio. You really get that creative tension going . . .

Docksey   New concept album: Dub Torture, featuring Dex on vocals!

He looks at **Dex** *contemptuously.*

This is an auld recording studio ya daft cunt. Or have you no noticed? (*He sweeps his hand around the room.*) Scream aw ye want. Naebodies gaunny hear ye.

Jinks   I'll phone his slag back in a minute, tell her a Mister Docherty will be looking after her.

Docksey   Very good, my man. Listen, Jinks, I still think we should put baby's gag in. I want to be there when he spraffs his first real words.

Jinks   Oh, no, Docks. You're seein Laney, so it's only fair that Dex and I should get to know each other.

Turns to **Dex**.

How does that sound to you, Dex? Chinese?

Dex   Just leave ays.

Docksey   That sounded quite coy there, Jinks. I think you're making an impression.

Dex   Help!

Jinks *and* **Docksey** *improvise the Beatles 'Help!'.*

Jinks Ah need somebody!

Docksey Help!

Jinks No just any fucker . . .

Docksey Help!

Jinks Ye ken ah need some cunt . . .

Jinks/Docksey He-eh-eh-eh-elp!

Jinks When ah wis younger, so much younger than today . . . ah used tae think that Dex here, wis such an easy lay . . .

Docksey (*sings*) Ooh ah ooh ah . . .

Jinks But now those days I find he's not so self-assured . . . I'm gonna fuck him from behind, and open his back door . . .

Jinks/Docksey (*singing, then collapsing into laughter*) Help him if you can . . . ha ha ha . . .

Docksey *then thrusts his hips.*

Docksey You goat me aw horny talking about fuckin here. (*Adopts game-show host's voice.*) It's time for a shag, so let's contact the slag . . .

Docksey *makes a phone gesture at* **Jinks**, *who heads to the control area.*

Dex Youse cunts!!

Jinks *plays it back with reverb.*

Scene Three

Laney *is at the flat. She is in the bedroom, looking through her wardrobe. There are a lot of expensive clothes in it. She pulls out a long, black, satin dress.*

Laney I've got this . . . and these (*Pulls out shoes.*) and these . . . (*Starts pulling out other clothes in a frenzy.*) and I've got fuck all!

She throws the clothes around and then moves over to the dressing table and throws all the perfumes on the floor.

I've got nothing! Nothing at all!

*She moves over to the picture of her and **Dex**. She sits down and lights up a cigarette.*

I've nothing tae dae wi your fuckin business! Ah dinnae even want tae know what your fuckin business is! Ah dinnae want tae fuckin know!

She trashes the bedroom a bit more, then collapses on to the bed in tears. The doorbell rings and she rushes through but does not open it.

Who is it?

Docksey (*shouting through door*)   Alan Docherty's the name. Did Jinks phone you?

Laney   Aye, c'moan in.

Docksey *enters.*

Docksey   Hiya.

Laney   Hiya.

Docksey   Laney, right?

Laney   Aye.

Docksey   Listen, ah'm sorry tae hear aboot yir felly. Ah mind ah met yis one time up the toon. Ah'd worked down south wi him once, but he didnae mind ay me. Remember?

Laney   Eh . . . aye, ah think so. Did ye know him?

Docksey   No very well. Him and Jinks were supposed tae be working the gither last night. Ah just worked wi him once on a delivery, a while back now.

Laney   Drugs?

Docksey   Naw, it wisnae drugs.

Laney   And even if it wis ye wouldnae say right?

Docksey *shrugs.*

Laney Do ye think he's deid?

Docksey Really, ah dunno what the score is . . .

Laney Ye think the ones that goat him are after me?

Docksey Ah wid doubt it, but yir better safe than sorry. Listen . . . ah dinnae ken how much eh telt ye aboot what we dae . . .

Laney Nowt, eh never telt me nowt.

Docksey Well in our game ye sometimes make enemies.

Laney Ah wis even thinkin ay callin the polis, but that guy Jinks said . . .

Docksey Listen, Laney . . . it isnae often ah agree wi Jinks, but dinnae git the polis involved, whatever ye dae. If Tyrone or any ay the top boys find oot you've done that . . .

Laney Right . . . but ah've nae money . . . ah've no goat any food in . . . eh left ays wi nae money. Ah don't know whae tae borrow some fae doon here . . .

Docksey *ostentatiously pulls out his wallet and peels off five hundred pounds from a big wad.*

Docksey Take this the now.

Laney Ye sure?

Docksey Course ah am.

Laney Thanks . . . Alan, is it?

Docksey That's it.

Laney Thanks, Alan.

He smiles and looks around.

Docksey Nice place.

Laney No when yuv been stuck in it waitin by the phone it isnae.

Docksey   Ah kin imagine. Look, they telt me tae make sure that you're okay. One thing ah want ye tae believe is that as long as ah'm here, nothing's gaunny happen tae you.

He gives her a deep, searching look.

Ye git that?

Laney   Aye . . .

Docksey   You were saying ye didnae have any food in. You hud anything tae eat lately?

Laney   Naw.

Docksey   Well, ah'll go oot and git a takeaway. Any news and Jinks'll bell ays oan the mobby. Dinnae open the door until ah git back.

Laney   Awright . . . God . . . ah'm a mess. Ah'm just gaunny go through and pit ma face oan.

Docksey   Looks okay tae me the way it is.

Laney *stares at* **Docksey** *a bit and then smiles.*

Docksey   Looks even better now!

Laney's *smile opens up even more, almost in spite of herself.*

Laney   Aye . . . right . . . ah'll go n get ready.

Docksey   Right. Ah'll git the gear.

Laney   Thir's a Chinky at the bottom ay the road . . .

Docksey   Ah'll see what there is.

He goes to depart but turns to face **Laney** *again.*

Mind, keep the door locked. Okay.

Laney   Okay.

Docksey *exits.*

Scene Four

Dex *is in the studio chained up.* **Jinks** *returns with some Chinese food.*

Dex What the fuck dae youse cunts want wi me ... this is some test ... Tyrone's giein ays some kind ay test. Well, ah'll tell youse cunts fuck all.

Jinks *is completely ignoring him.*

Dex Fuck all!
Dex Murray!

Jinks *lays the cartons out on the table.*

Jinks Lemon chick-on ... flied lice ... barbecue spa-ah libs ...

Dex Ah'm fuckin strong!

Jinks ... spling lolls ...

Dex Ah'll no fuckin crack!

Jinks ... king plawn with gleen peppah and black bean sauce ...

Dex Tyrone'll see that!

Jinks ... this is going to be a banquet fit for a king ... and a queen.

Turns to **Dex**.

I hope you like it spicy.

Dex This hus gone far enough, mate. Ah'm no jokin.

Jinks You should joke a bit mair. You're too uptight. Relax.

Goes over to **Dex** *and starts tickling him.*

Whoah ho ... whoah ho ...

Dex Fuck off!

Jinks Oohhh. Wide boy! Would you like a spring roll, wide boy?

Dex *says nothing, but is obviously hungry.*

Jinks   I take it that's a yes.

Dex   Take it any way ye want tae.

Jinks   Mmmm ... you're a saucy one all right. Now
listen, if I give you a spring roll, what will you give me?
What will ah get in return?

Dex   Fuck off ya poof! Keep away fae me.

Jinks *goes up to* **Dex** *and makes out that he is going to kiss him.*

Jinks   Kissy kissy ...

Dex   Fuck off!

Jinks *then tweaks* **Dex**'*s nipples with the pliers.*

Dex   Dinnae! Dinnae! Aaaghhhh!

Jinks *relaxes his grip with the pliers.*

Jinks   I'm going to have to do your gag.

Dex   Naw ... dinnae ...

Jinks   Yes, I will. Basically, just because I can.

He starts to do up **Dex**'*s gag.* **Dex**'*s struggle is now more resigned
and half-hearted.* **Jinks** *puts a set of headphones on* **Dex** *and
secures them with tape.*

Jinks (*sings*)   Music was my first love ...

He goes to the control desk and turns up the volume switch. **Dex**
flinches in silent agony.

... and it will be my last ...

Scene Five

Laney *has put on a bit of make up. The doorbell goes.*

Laney   Who is it?

It is **Docksey** *with the takeaway.*

Docksey   Alan.

Laney *opens the door.* **Docksey** *looks at her, obviously impressed. He moves into the flat.*

Docksey   Bonjour, Madame . . . we have olives, sun-dried tomatoes, salads, a selection of cheeses . . .

Laney *looks a bit doubtful.*

Laney   Did ye no go tae the Chinky but?

Docksey   Naw . . . that sort ay stuffs bad fir ye. Ah like tae look after masel. Good food, good wine, aw that sort ay thing.

Laney   Ah've never hud this kind ay stuff before. Dex didnae . . .

Laney *hesitates.*

Docksey   Look, ah didnae ken the boy really, but he wis your boyfriend and I'm really sorry aboot all the distress this must've caused you. Ah mean, talk aboot it if ye want.

Laney *looks hostile.*

Docksey   If ye dinnae want tae though, dinnae. Ah mean, ah'm here tae make sure that you're awright.

Laney   Mibee we should talk aboot you.

Docksey   Isnae that interesting.

Laney *looks at him doubtfully.* **Docksey** *starts getting the food on to plates. He pours the wines into glasses.* **Laney** *helps him and they sit down to eat.*

Laney   Ah'll no ask ye what ye do.

Docksey   Someday ah'll tell ye. But what aboot you? What is it you do?

Laney   Nowt . . . well . . . ah used tae work as a receptionist in a hotel . . . ah wanted tae go tae college, tae dae a course in design.

Docksey   That sounds cool. What do ye no go fir?

Laney   Dex. He said it was a waste ay time. He made enough money.

Docksey   Quite a traditional attitude.

Laney   That the way he wis . . . is, eh.

Docksey   Takes all sorts, ah suppose.

Laney   You dinnae seem a traditional kind.

Docksey   Naw it's just that ah think that education's important . . . ah mean, ah started this Open University course a few years back. Did the foundation course in Humanities. Enjoyed it. I'd like tae get back intae it again. Too busy though, that's the problem.

Laney   In your line ay work!

Docksey   Aye . . .

He pours some wine.

Ah'll tell ye what aboot yir felly though: if ah had such a beautiful lady tae come back tae, ah widnae be disappearing in a hurry.

Laney *looks angry for a while, then smiles at bit.* **Docksey** *raises his glass.*

Docksey   Ah meant that as a compliment. Sorry if it was a bit insensitive.

Laney   It's awright. Ah'll take it as a compliment.

Docksey   Great. Cheers!

Laney   Cheers.

Scene Six

Back at the studio. **Jinks** *is stripped to the waist and wearing tracksuit bottoms and boxing gloves. He is 'sparring' with* **Dex**, *stopping the punches short, as* **Docksey** *enters.*

Jinks Docksey! How are ye! (*Adopts posh Edinburgh 'Morningside' accent.*) You'll hev hed your hole! Tell us the gory details about you and that Laney slag. I'm sure Dex here is just fuckin well dying tae ken!

Docksey You've got him gagged!

Jinks Unfortunately Dex abused the freedom I secured for him. He said some hurtful things.

Docksey What's the sounds Dex is listening tae?

Jinks Ah pit Engelbert Humperdink's 'Please Release Me' oan the loop. Eh must be getting a wee bit sick ay it by now. Take them oaf. I'm sure he wants tae hear the sordid details of your cock-a-leekie and a certain hoor's orifices.

Docksey *looks a wee bit doubtful, but takes the taped headphones from* **Dex***'s head.* **Dex** *looks bleary and disorientated.*

Docksey Hello, Mister Murray!

He looks at **Jinks**.

You in training?

Jinks (*stretching*) Yeah, ah felt masel gettin a wee bit tight.

Docksey No goat a punchbag set up?

Jinks (*looks at* **Dex**) Oh, ah certainly have. N ah've goat a ring as well . . .

Moves around **Dex** *and looks at his arse.*

. . . n ah intend tae cover every inch ay it.

He goes round and starts dancing and mock-sparring with **Dex**, *stopping the punches short. He turns to* **Docksey**.

You gaunny tell ays how ye got on wi this Laney hoor?

Docksey All in good time. First, I want to fill in Dex with a bit of background. Mind how we went doon the garage that time, Jinks, whaire they selt the records? All those years ago. Funny how a wee visit to a garage can map out your whole destiny.

Jinks *is breathing in slightly distressed manner.* **Docksey** *notes this.*

Docksey Ye awright, mate? Take it easy, eh.

Jinks Ah'm fine.

Docksey Ye sure?

Jinks Ah said so, didn't ah?

Docksey *shrugs.* **Jinks** *turns to* **Dex**.

Jinks That was it, twelve years auld and our destiny mapped right out. Crazy, eh sweetheart?

Docksey That was us, Dex. Mind you, you would've just been in primary then.

Jinks Cute in your shorts, ah'll bet. A wee cock tease even then, eh?

Docksey Thing wis, Dex, it wis aw an accident. Mind we were just hingin aboot the garage, checkin oot the records, deciding on what single tae buy. T. Rex 'Easy Action' you wanted, eh Jinks.

Jinks Solid Gold Easy Action.

To **Dex** *in English middle-class DJ accent.*

Solid Gold.

Docksey Thing is Henry Logan comes over. You'll ken Logan, eh no, Dex? At least by reputation. We're twelve and Logan's sixteen. Another fuckin world. We're shitein oor fuckin keks, eh Jinks?

Jinks (*to* **Dex**) Frightened, but excited n aw. Ken the feeling, angel heart?

Docksey Well, Logan's collectin for Fat Tyrone who's goat this huge fine tae pey oaf or it's the nick for him. Tyrone wisnae as discreet as he is now. Well, Dex, two young laddies, shitein it, we just hands over our cash. So no 'Easy Action' for us pair, eh, Jinks.

Jinks   Mibbe git some easy action wi you though, eh sweetheart?

Docksey   That would be nice though, eh Jinks, if me and Laney and you and Dex got it the gither. No think so, Dex? Ah would say that would be the dream ticket. That's the plan.

Jinks (*singing*)   I thought he was a shy boy ... ooh ah ... ah aahh ... until I made him my boy ... ooh ah aaah ah ...

Docksey   Well, this cunt Logan, he only wants me n Jinks here tae collect for Tyrone. So what could we say but 'Certainly sir' or words tae that effect.

Jinks   And we collected like fuck. Enterprise, angel heart, we showed we had it. Fag rackets, jumble sales, Subbuteo and table tennis competitions, five-a-side tourneys up the centre ... we raised aboot twenty quid ... when it wis twenty quid.

Docksey   Wisnae twenty, Jinks ...

Jinks   Fuckin wis ...

Docksey   Nearer fifteen.

Jinks   Awright, but that wis near enough a ton in these days.

Docksey   Aye, and this is twelve years auld we're talkin aboot. So we're chuffed and ready tae take the cash roond tae Logan. We kept a bit back for ourselves for singles. Thing wis that Logan's been sent doon in the meantime, he's banged up in Polmont, the daft cunt. So there's us sittin oan this dosh. Dosh that nearly every cunt kens we've been collectin for Fat Tyrone.

Jinks   Somebody's frightened now. Fat Tyrone, eh!

*He feels **Dex**'s arse.*

It's poopy, poopy panties.

Docksey   Fancy a pill, Jinks?

Jinks Doves?

Docksey Aye.

Jinks A little of what you fancy does you no harm at all.

He has his gloves on, so **Docksey** *drops it into his mouth.* **Jinks** *starts to dance.*

Ah think that ah'm a reincarnation ay Marie Lloyd.

He turns to **Dex** *and punches him.*

Who're you fuckin lookin at? Nae cunts fuckin well talkin tae you!

Docksey (*in American voice to* **Dex**) Say, Dex, I guess that must smart.

Jinks It's always when you dinnae expect it that the pain's the highest. I know you're tied up, angel heart, but you can still move your heid. You have to be on your guard here, dollface; alert at aw fuckin times, I dunno if you follow the fight game but you must remember Herrol Graham, the Sheffield-based boxer? What reflexes that cunt had. He used to go into a pub with hands tied behind his back and bet that nae cunt could hit him. The speed that that boy moved his heid. You try, dollface.

He swings at **Dex** *and hits him.*

Jinks Awww . . .

Docksey Too slow, Dex. Mind, that's what happened tae perr auld Herrol. They caught the cunt once, and once was enough.
Anywey, we digress. What was ah sayin? Aye! We had tae take the dosh roond tae Fat Tyrone's hoose. We wir fuckin shakin.

Jinks Tyrone's ma let us in. Tyrone's in the kitchen, drinkin tea and gettin wired intae a big plate ay bacon and egg rolls. Fat cunt even then, eh.

Docksey The cunt just looks aroond at these two squeaky wee laddies. Ah jist says, we've goat some money we collected. Fir the fine. Ah pit it oan the table. 'Where did yis git this?' he goes. So we telt him. Mind, Jinks?

Jinks   Aye. We goes: Logan said ye needed it, so we collected it. Set up a Tyrone Power fund. Loads ay people pit in. We hud tournaments at the centre, the lot, we sais tae the cunt. Mind the look oan his face? It was worth giein the cunt the dosh.

Docksey   Aw aye. Now you ken Tyrone, Dex. Course ye do.

Jinks   Everybody knows him. David Alexander Power. Fat-fucking-Ty-fucking-Rone.

Docksey   N once ye stop playing silly cunts yill tell us aw aboot him.

Jinks   A mair vicious cunt never lived, but the thing is, the tears wir wellin up in his eyes.

Docksey   Reminded ays ay the general in *White Christmas* when Bing Crosby and Danny Kaye had set up the big do for him.

Jinks   I love that film.

Docksey   He wis only aboot twenty, though that wis ancient tae us. A young buck on his way up, no the main man yit. But the daft cunt had this sentimental streak, he had this fantasy that a loat ay the auld school ay nutters entertain; namely that he was loved and respected by the community.

Jinks   And he was so touched at what he saw as them rallying roond tae keep his blubbery erse oot ay the slammer. (*Impersonates Tyrone.*) 'See if any cunt ever messes wi you boys . . .'

Jinks gestures at **Docksey** *to help him remove the gloves, which he does.*

Docksey   That wis the cunt right enough. Fat Tyrone was moved. Twelve years auld and we were in. Hud hardly had a proper wank and thair wi wir walkin roond wi bags ay skag in oor pockits: home deliveries. Too young for the jail see; that wis Tyrone's scam. Never caught though, eh, Jinks?

Jinks   We're so good at being undetected . . .

Docksey   Thing is, Dex, you ken the score in this game, you mair than any cunt. Wir flush by schemie standards, but it's just fuckin trinket money. As we git intae oor teens and leave school we've goat the clathes n the motor. No enough dosh but for the gaff up the toon. Ah ken you managed that, Dex, nice one.

He looks at **Dex** *who looks embarrassed.*

Normally though, they like tae keep ye in the fuckin scheme, oan yir ain patch. That's whair ye dae the biz. Push the collies.

Jinks   Push the collies . . . that's a load ay shite, eh.

Docksey   Aw aye, push the fuckin collies. Ye push fuck all. The only cunts that push drugs are the brewers and tobacconists, Dex, these cunts that are sponsored by the state, that have to advertise their inferior products. It's a typical state operation, like the auld commie countries tryin tae sell thir crap motors that nae cunt wants.

Jinks   We ken that for our superior products in the private sector, demand always exceeds supply. We dinnae huv tae push, the cunts are beatin a fuckin path tae yir door.

Docksey   Aye, the biggest problem is keeping the customer discreet. That's what fucked me, Dex. Three years for possession ay two hundred and fifty eckies. Some cunt blabbed.

He looks at **Dex**.

That's another tale though. The point ah'm makin is that once yir in, some cunt always wants ye tae dae mair.

Jinks *starts to undo* **Dex**'s *gag. He has the pliers on him.*

Docksey You ken aw this, now you fuckin well tell us. You fuckin speak.

Dex Ma fuckin ears ... you bastards ...

He looks at **Docksey**.

... ah dinnae ken what your game is, mate, but you should ken the fuckin score. You're makin a big mistake ...

Jinks *pinches* **Dex**'s *nipples with the pliers*. **Dex** *screams in agony*.

Jinks Shut yir fuckin mooth cunt!

Docksey Whoops, caught again, Dex.

Jinks Want ays tae really fuckin dae ye? Eh! Want ays tae take yir fuckin teeth oot?

Dex Nup ...

Jinks Speak fuckin nice then ya fuckin bag ay shite or ah'll cut of your fuckin baws, stick them in the microwave, droon the cunts in broon sauce and scran them doon right in front ay ye!

Jinks *starts to hyperventilate*.

Docksey Take it easy, mate.

Jinks Aye ...

Docksey Calm doon. Dinnae git wired. Take it easy. Pill's kickin in, eh.

Jinks Aye ...

Docksey (*to* **Dex**) N you, dae as the man says. Speak nice.

Dex What dae yis want ays tae fuckin say?

Docksey Tell us aboot yirsel. Yir life.

Dex You ken that isnae oan ... you ken the score.

Jinks I don't think you fuckin well realise just what the situ is, sweetheart. Will ah tell ye what's gaunny happen?

Docksey You don't fuckin threaten us. You talk and you fuckin listen. Right!

Dex Right ...

Jinks Docksey here's gaunny git your burd, Laney is it? He's gaunny fuck her goodstyle, eh Docksey?

Docksey *does not respond but looks at* **Dex**.

Dex Look ... keep her oot ay this ... she's fuck all tae dae wi anything. Right?

Docksey You keep her oot ay it! You fuckin talk!

Jinks But that's the least ay your worries, cause ah'm gaunny fuck you right up your wee laddie's erse. Dig?

Dex Keep away fi me!

Jinks The thing is, that eftir ah dae that, then ah fuckin well turn really nasty. So does Docksey. So fuckin nasty dae we turn that what you'll dae is long for the time when ah wis only fuckin yir erse.

Docksey You'll genuinely look back on these lovemaking sessions with Jinks wi some fanciful nostalgia, Dex. You'll plead for these days to return. Oh yes, you will. But they willnae, Dex. But that's you.

He walks away, laughing and shaking his head.

It looks rosier for me. I got a wee kiss from Laney the other night, mate. I think I could've lingered, could've tried to slip in a wee bit of tongue, a light feel of the erse maybe, but I didnae. That would be your style: the ungentlemanly style. Tonight though, perhaps.

Dex Fuckin leave her ya dirty sick cunts!

Jinks *punches* **Dex** *and they secure the gag.*

Docksey I'll give it tae Dex, he's done no bad. Still refusing to co-operate. Thinks we'll let him go eftir a few days. Doesnae realise that this is him for the rest of his puff.

Jinks   But that might not be a long time.

Docksey   I think he's trying to turn you on. All that anger, all those threats, that snarling.

Jinks   I've never been able to resist machismo.

Docksey *holds* **Dex** *while* **Jinks** *takes off his trousers.*

Jinks   Mmmm . . . I never took you for a boxer shorts man. Pretty disappointing. I prefer briefs . . . just because they're so, well . . . brief, I suppose.
Relax, my little darling. I'm not going to fuck you yet. Luckily for you I've made this pact that I can't until Docksey's ready to do your bird. (*To* **Docksey**.) So you're wooing for two.

Docksey   Nae bother tae Docksey. We'll have a joint wedding!

Jinks   Fuckin right . . . but listen, one thing ah want you tae realise. George Benson was the first ever guitarist tae record wi Miles Davis.

Docksey   Gen up?

Jinks   Aye. So think aboot that before ye start aw this George Benson disco-handbags shite.

Docksey   Hmm . . . interesting . . . if it's gen.

Jinks   Too right it's fuckin gen.

Docksey   Awright, ah'll take yir word for it. In the meantime, let's show our little friend some slides to jog his memory.

Docksey *and* **Jinks** *set up a screen and projector.* **Docksey** *takes a red folder and stands in front of* **Dex**. *He speaks in a put-on Irish accent.*

Derek More-ay, dis is your loife. Sorry aboot the Eamonn Andrews thair, Dex, but ah cannae dae that Michael Aspel cunt. Anyway, you were born in a shitey scheme in a shitey city in a shitey coontray and grew oop a roight fughin wanker. Do you recognise dis face?

Jinks *flashes up a picture on the screen, it is a picture of a man with glasses. They study* **Dex**'s *reaction.*

Jinks Ah'd say 'yes'.

Docksey Aw aye, he kens that boy awright, we baith do, eh, Dex? Study that picture, Dex. We'll talk later. Jinks, fancy choppin oot a line ay posh?

Jinks Sound.

He is at the table and starts chopping out lines of cocaine.

Remember that imortal line in *Basic Instinct*, the film?

Docksey That big ride, that Sharon Stone shag, mind ay what she sais tae that Michael Douglas cunt?

Jinks (*to* **Dex**, *in American accent*) Ever fucked on coke?

Docksey We'll fuckin well find oot your Basic Instinct, Dex, fuckin sure'n we will!
But of course . . . ye dinnae want tae talk. Okay, that's cool. Well, ah'll tell the fuckin story.

Jinks Ah'd love tae hear it.

Darkness falls as they snort the lines.

The darkened stage is illuminated by a spotlight on **Docksey**, *who is at the front of the stage, and one on* **Dex** *and* **Jinks**, *to the rear. In the background there is large screen which flashes up slide images.*

The image which flashes up is a shot of a family, a man, a woman and two young girls.

Docksey *looks at this image and is pained.* **Dex** *looks away.*
Jinks *is intrigued.*

Docksey You didnae ken his family, did ye, Dex?

Another slide flashes up, this time it is just the man.

Colin. Colin Barraclough. Nice guy. Mind the night oot we had wi him, Dex?

Dex *is silent.*

Docksey A nice guy, but he had a problem. Couldnae pass a bookie. Tried everything; just couldnae pass one. Horses mainly, but duqs n aw. Fruit machines, casinos, scratch-cairds . . . you name it. Of course, he had tae pey for his pleasure when the creditors started knocking on the door. You always need tae borrow tae keep it gaun. Then, eventually, ye borrow fae the wrong cunts.

Another slide flashes up. It is a picture of a man.

There he is . . . big Davie Power.

Jinks Fat Tyrone. No bad photae ay the fat cunt but eh.

Another slide flashes up. It is a leaner-looking man.

Docksey Jamieson. You mind ay that cunt, Dex? Alisdair Jamieson. He brought us together on Tyrone's behalf.

Dex *is silent.*

Docksey Those cunts dinnae need the five grand this boy owed them. Sweeties tae thaim. Thing is, their credibility depends on them no getting the pish takin ooat ay them by guys like perr Colin. The vanishing of a debtor is good for business.

Jinks The other debtors cough up quick eftir that. They dinnae want kidnapped by the aliens.

Docksey So Tyrone and Jamieson send for two aliens tae take perr Colin away from the bosom of his loving family.

A slide of **Dex** *flashes up, followed by one of* **Docksey**.

Jinks That was a nice one of you, angel heart. Caught your good side.

Docksey But they fucked up. They sent two cunts from the same city doon tae Sheffield. Tyrone and Jamieson got their wires crossed. They sent two cunts that could get tae know each other, that had a lot ay the same acquaintances.

Jinks Tsk tsk . . . careless.

Docksey But it was worse than that. They sent two fuckin novices n aw. Oan the train doon, ah thought this cunt wis the big hit man. Ah had tae pit up wi aw his bullshit tellin ays how eh wis gaunny do this guy. Ah should've realised eh wis too mouthy tae be a real pro, but ah jist took um for an enthusiastic psycho who loved ehs job.

He laughs.

Well, we went doon thaire, met Colin at the dug track. Got him half-bevied and took him back tae this flat we'd rented. He was having the time ay his life n aw, the perr cunt. He goes tae the bogs n ah says tae Dex here, ah goes tae try n gie him the hammer, ah goes: lit the cunt have it! Ken what this cunt says?

Jinks Do tell . . .

Docksey This cunt, the cunt wi the mooth, eh says, you dae it, you've goat the hammer. This is ma first time, eh sais. Ah look at him. Eh goes: ah thoat ah wis here tae watch you, like a biscuit-ersed bairn . . .

Jinks *goes up to* **Dex** *and pinches his cheek.*

Jinks Aw didums . . . (*Sings.*) If I had a hammer . . .

Docksey *shakes his head and paces the stage, before turning to the audience and looking skywards.*

Docksey . . . and this Colin cunt comes back, and ehs sittin oan the couch and ehs gaun oan aboot how he's never hud such a good time in ages n aboot his wife and bairns and ah'm standin above him and ah dinnae ken what tae dae and ma hands are shakin and ah bring the hammer doon oan his heid and there's a crack and again and again and he's falling forward oaf the couch and ah'm oantae him, hitting him again and again and his heid cracking open like a walnut and there's blood everywhere and Dex's oan his back wi the flex fae the lamp aroond his neck and hes throttlin the cunt . . .

. . . just fuckin die! Ah scream at um. Jist fuckin well let go!

And Dex's fuckin sayin, bash ehs fuckin nut right in! Drive the hammer right intae it!

And ah'm wantin um tae die, tae let go, the cunt's brains are mashin under ma hammer, ah'm drivin it right intae the grey matter and this cunt here's shoutin: ah'll choke ye ya cunt! Dex Murray's ma name!

Then the boy goes intae his death throes; pishin, shitein and twitchin . . . and it's over.

Jinks *starts to massage the back of* **Docksey**'s *neck.*

Docksey   Ah'm sittin thair in his blood, ah cannae move, ah'm nearly as deid as the cunt himself. Ah never thought that it would be like that . . . it took so long, man. Eh widnae lit go. The boy widnae lit go.

He points at **Dex**.

Dex here but, he's jumpin aroond like he's scored the winnin goal in a cup final . . . no that, as a jambo, Dex, you'd ken much aboot winnin goals in cup finals . . .

Jinks *claws the air in a bitchy gesture.*

Docksey   . . . we did it though, he's gaun: we did it! You n me! We fuckin well offed the cunt! Fuckin wasted um! Ah'm saying that we shouldnae have man, we shouldnae have done that . . .
Shut up, Dex says. It's fuckin done now. We did it!
What did we dae?

Another slide, the man in a pool of blood.

That picture was the one I took for Tyrone.
Then we wrapped him up in the carpet. The boys are thorough in the morning. They take him up in the carpet, sand the flairs, the fuckin lot.
What dae they dae wi the boady?
You never know. You know that it willnae be found though.

He walks towards **Dex**.

The whole thing fucked ma heid. Ah want tae hear your fuckin story!

*He takes out **Dex***'s gag.*

We topped that poor cunt for his debts of five fuckin grand.

He flashes up the slide of the dead man with his wife and children.

He had a wife and two wee daughters. We killed them. We removed a husband and a father from the world for five thousand pounds of a stupid, ugly, fat rich cunt's money.

*He points to **Dex**.*

And this cunt here just danced aroond like a wee laddie that had scored a fuckin goal in the cup final.

Dex *looks hard at him.*

Dex   Ah'm sayin nowt...

Docksey   We got a miserable fuckin two grand each. They thought that one guy vanishing for good would set an example for other debtors. They were right, I suppose. How dae ye feel aboot that now?

Dex   It's done. It wis business.

Docksey   Ah feel shite. Always did. Ah mind when ah went tae jail, for dealin the pills, ah thought aboot it a lot. Funny, when a got sent tae jail, ah just thought, maybe a bit ay Karma eh. But ah thought aboot Colin and his family a lot. No much else tae dae, eh. Didnae want tae, but ah couldnae stoap. Did the Open Uni Foundation course. Art, history, moral philosophy.

Ah've goat a wee fuckin moral proposition for ye, Dex: unless you're a psychopath, unless you're really damaged, then you take consequences for yir actions. Ye huv tae. What dae ye say tae that?

Dex   So what gives you the right tae dae this tae me? You wir the one...

Docksey What gies me the right is thit ah've hud shite.
In here.

He taps his head.

You've no convinced me thit you've hud shite. If ye huv,
tell ays aboot it. If ye huvnae, tell ays how no. Right?

Dex You ken wi cannae talk . . .

Docksey Fuckin well thinks eh's MI5, eh. Well ah'll tell
you something; when ah goat oot the nick ah went doon
thair, went tae see the boy's wife and kids. Didnae make
contact likes, just watched them. Those lives that we'd
fucked up, just like we'd fucked up his that night.
Ah took the consequences. Ah gave up oan life. Then ah
started tae think aboot you, mate. Wonder how that boy's
coped, ah thought.

Dex Ye huv tae. It's the wey it is. It's what ye dae.
You're in the game as much as ah am. You should fuckin
well ken!

Docksey Still the hard cunt, wi that disengaged
professional spiel. Ah'm trying tae get beyond it, Dex.
Ah'm tryin tae work oot if that's aw thir is tae ye, or is
there some other reason you can cope, something else
which makes it easier for you.
Maybe Laney holds the key.

Dex Listen tae me, mate, she's goat nowt tae dae wi
anything. Just leave her oot ay it.

Jinks *moves around* **Dex**.

Jinks It's awright, ignore Docksey. He's just a bit ay a
sensitive cunt. If you dinnae want tae git intae aw that wi
him, it's nae fuckin bother. Ah like a frivolous wee fun boy.
Ah dinnae care if it's love yir eftir, or jist a good time.
When ah'm stickin it up your erse ah dinnae care whether
or no you sob like a wee lassie or buck like a wild stallion.
Ah'm still pumpin plenty fuckin muck intae your rectum!

Docksey Rectum?

METHUEN SCREENPLAYS

☐ BEAUTIFUL THING	Jonathan Harvey	£6.99
☐ THE ENGLISH PATIENT	Anthony Minghella	£7.99
☐ THE CRUCIBLE	Arthur Miller	£6.99
☐ THE WIND IN THE WILLOWS	Terry Jones	£7.99
☐ PERSUASION	Jane Austen, adapted by Nick Dear	£6.99
☐ TWELFTH NIGHT	Shakespeare, adapted by Trevor Nunn	£7.99
☐ THE KRAYS	Philip Ridley	£7.99
☐ THE AMERICAN DREAMS (THE REFLECTING SKIN & THE PASSION OF DARKLY NOON)	Philip Ridley	£8.99
☐ MRS BROWN	Jeremy Brock	£7.99
☐ THE GAMBLER	Dostoyevsky, adapted by Nick Dear	£7.99
☐ TROJAN EDDIE	Billy Roche	£7.99
☐ THE WINGS OF THE DOVE	Hossein Amini	£7.99
☐ THE ACID HOUSE TRILOGY	Irvine Welsh	£8.99
☐ THE LONG GOOD FRIDAY	Barrie Keeffe	£6.99
☐ SLING BLADE	Billy Bob Thornton	£7.99

METHUEN DRAMA
MONOLOGUE & SCENE BOOKS

☐ CONTEMPORARY SCENES FOR ACTORS (MEN)	Earley and Keil	£8.99
☐ CONTEMPORARY SCENES FOR ACTORS (WOMEN)	Earley and Keil	£8.99
☐ THE CLASSICAL MONOLOGUE (MEN)	Earley and Keil	£7.99
☐ THE CLASSICAL MONOLOGUE (WOMEN)	Earley and Keil	£7.99
☐ THE CONTEMPORARY MONOLOGUE (MEN)	Earley and Keil	£7.99
☐ THE CONTEMPORARY MONOLOGUE (WOMEN)	Earley and Keil	£7.99
☐ THE MODERN MONOLOGUE (MEN)	Earley and Keil	£7.99
☐ THE MODERN MONOLOGUE (WOMEN)	Earley and Keil	£7.99
☐ THE METHUEN AUDITION BOOK FOR MEN	Annika Bluhm	£6.99
☐ THE METHUEN AUDITION BOOK FOR WOMEN	Annika Bluhm	£6.99
☐ THE METHUEN AUDITION BOOK FOR YOUNG ACTORS	Anne Harvey	£6.99
☐ THE METHUEN BOOK OF DUOLOGUES FOR YOUNG ACTORS	Anne Harvey	£6.99

● All Methuen Drama books are available through mail order or from your local bookshop.

Please send cheque/eurocheque/postal order (sterling only) Access, Visa, Mastercard, Diners Card, Switch or Amex.

☐☐☐☐☐☐☐☐☐☐☐☐☐☐☐☐

Expiry Date:_____ Signature: _____

Please allow 75 pence per book for post and packing U.K.
Overseas customers please allow £1.00 per copy for post and packing.

ALL ORDERS TO:

Methuen Books, Books by Post, TBS Limited, The Book Service, Colchester Road, Frating Green, Colchester, Essex CO7 7DW.

NAME: _____

ADDRESS: _____

_____

_____

Please allow 28 days for delivery. Please tick box if you do not wish to receive any additional information   ☐

Prices and availability subject to change without notice.